The Underground Cabaret

Also by Ian Seed

Anonymous Intruder (Shearsman Books, 2009)
Shifting Registers (Shearsman Books, 2011)
Makers of Empty Dreams (Shearsman Books, 2014)
Identity Papers (Shearsman Books, 2016)
New York Hotel (Shearsman Books, 2018)

Chapbooks

Threadbare Fables (Like This Press, 2012)
Sleeping with the Ice Cream Vendor (Knives, Forks and Spoons Press, 2012)
Fidelities (Red Ceilings Press, 2015)

Translations

No One Else at Home (from the Polish of Joanna Skalska) (Flax, 2007)
the straw which comes apart (from the Italian of Ivano Fermini) (Oystercatcher Press, 2010)
The Thief of Talant (from the French of Pierre Reverdy) (Wakefield Press, 2016)
Bitter Grass (from the Italian of Gëzim Hajdari) (Shearsman Books, 2020)

Fiction

Amore mio (Flaxebooks, 2010)
Italian Lessons (Like This Press, 2017)

Ian Seed

The Underground Cabaret

Shearsman Books

First published in the United Kingdom in 2020 by
Shearsman Books Ltd
PO Box 4239
Swindon
SN3 9FN

Shearsman Books Ltd Registered Office
30–31 St. James Place, Mangotsfield, Bristol BS16 9JB
(this address not for correspondence)

www.shearsman.com

ISBN 978-1-84861-723-0

Copyright © Ian Seed, 2020.
The right of Ian Seed to be identified as the author
of this work has been asserted by him in accordance with the
Copyrights, Designs and Patents Act of 1988.
All rights reserved.

ACKNOWLEDGEMENTS

I am grateful to the editors of the following publications, where some of these poems first appeared, sometimes in different versions: *Anthropocene*; *Burning House*; *The Café Irreal*; *Distances* (a Red Ceilings limited-edition chapbook); *Flash: The International Short-Short Story Magazine*; *The Fortnightly Review*; *Free Verse: A Journal of Contemporary Poetry & Poetics*; *Granta magazine*; *Ink Sweat and Tears*; *International Times*; *Litter*; *Long Poem Magazine*; *Pandora's Box*; *Shearsman magazine*; *Stride*; *talking about strawberries all the time*; *Tears in the Fence*; and *Westerly* (Australia).

'Light' first appeared in the anthology, *Quartet: The Four Seasons*, ed. Deborah Gaye (Avalanche Books, 2018).

My thanks to Cassandra Atherton, Jeremy Over, Jane Monson, Justyna Raginia and to friends in the Lancaster writing group for support and helpful suggestions.

Infinite thanks to Tony Frazer.

Contents

Story	11
Working Late	12
Nostalgia	13
Missing	14
Fare	15
Labour	16
Division	17
Rome	18
Find	19
Provincial	20
Last Trip	21
Cottage	22
Youth	23
Morning After	24
Opening	25
Corridor	26
Care (1)	27
Old Town	28
Lesson	29
View	30
Loss	31
That Morning	32
Family Affair	33
Fields	34
Country Holiday	35
Pattern	36
Visitor	37
Patronage	38
Tunnel	39
Being Free	40
Lines	41
Interruption	42
Company (1)	43

Worth	44
Taint	45
Picnic	46
Verboten	47
Reception	48
Abuse	49
Translator	50
Job	51
Bad Breath	52
Inheritance	53
Precious	54
Need	55
Care (2)	56
Investment	57
The Unseen Everyday	58
Business	59
Distances	60
Survival	61
Together	62
Mauvaise Foi	63
Company (2)	64
Company (3)	65
Historical Movie	66
Want	67
Kiss	68
Arrival	69
The Order of Things	70
Spring Morning	71
Dialogue	72
Romance	73
Light	74
Hike	75
Daybreak	76
Incomplete	77
Poem	78

Destination	79
Separation	80
Invitation	81
In the Empty House	82
Mud, Gold	83
Recognition	84
Vita Nova	85
Good Behaviour	86
Voice	87
Telangiectasia	88
The Road to the City	89
Block	90
Soap	91
Differences	92
Carriage	93
Pet	94
Suits	95
Lock Keeper	96
Cry	97
Academic	98
Reading	99
Complicit	100
Illuminated	101
Game	102
New Friend	103
In My Absence	104
Work	105
Criteria	106

'Je suis donc fondé à dire que le sentiment de l'absurdité ne naît pas du simple examen d'un fait ou d'une impression mais qu'il jaillit de la comparaison entre un état de fait et une certaine réalité, entre une action et le monde qui la dépasse.'
—Albert Camus

'Positively there is no chair down here to offer you.'
—Joseph Conrad

Story

The steep stone steps led down to a restaurant in a cellar with long wooden tables and shelves stacked with dusty bottles of wine. Each evening a different dish was prepared, but only in limited quantities, and I wondered if I had arrived too late. I was the last customer to be allowed in.

At the end of the meal, straws were drawn to decide which one of us would perform that evening. It seemed inevitable the straw would come to me.

I took off my shirt and announced that with the point of my steak knife I would incise the story of the day into my skin, and then sing the events depicted there with improvised lyrics.

It was bound to be a distortion of the truth, but I hoped to make it seem authentic, not only for the sake of my reputation, but also in order not to break the spell of the stories which my audience told themselves to make their own lives real.

Working Late

I took the train to work that day as usual, even though I felt ill. I had my suitcase and rucksack with me because I would be staying overnight.

At the top of the escalator at St Pancras, I felt someone tugging at my rucksack. I turned around. The zip was open and some of my papers had fallen to the ground. A young man bent down and picked them up for me. He smiled but wouldn't look me in the eye.

I was the first one there for the department meeting, and was almost falling asleep when I felt a kiss on the back of my neck. It was my colleague S.

'Don't be alarmed,' she said. 'It's just that I think you do a wonderful job, and no one ever thanks you.'

I felt much worse now and left the room to get a pain-killer from my suitcase, but the suitcase was gone. Had it been stolen, or had I left it on the train?

The meeting went on for hours. When it was over, my boss offered to take me to the station on his way home to see if someone had found the suitcase.

He had a new, posh car.

It was hired, he said, explaining that he preferred a hired one so that he could exchange it whenever he wanted.

Wasn't that expensive? I wanted to know. He shook his head with a smile.

'Take care,' he said, when he dropped me off.

It was already night. The sky was dark and senseless.

Nostalgia

A terrible storm is brewing. Looking out of the window, I see the street has become dark in a way that makes it look like a scene from an old black-and-white film. A fine time to have to go into town. Walking through the park, all in black and white, I see a plump woman lying naked, like one of those on a fin-de-siècle postcard. She is so still she might not be alive. It is only when I realise that I can *will* colour back into the picture that the woman starts to move, and the terrible wind, which we are all at the mercy of, finally dies down.

Missing

I found the creature – a kind of horse dressed like a doll with her ears sticking out on either side of a bonnet, wearing rimless spectacles like an old granny, and talking to herself like a small child – walking on her back legs down the main thoroughfare of the great city. She was evidently quite lost. I put my arm around her waist – soft and furry like a teddy bear's – and led her home with me.

My wife wouldn't let me keep her, so I put an announcement in the local paper. A man from the other side of the city came to claim her. Something about him made me uneasy, and I followed him as he led the talking horse onto a tram and down through the rows to the back seat.

The horse was chattering away to herself quite happily and didn't seem to care whether I was there or not, so after giving her a last hug and saying goodbye once again, I got off the tram.

The tram-stop was in the middle of a dual-carriageway and the traffic swarmed by on either side. I realised I didn't have a clue where I was, and had no idea how to get back home.

Fare

I can't eat the sausages I've been given for breakfast. They are pink and fatty and smell funny. When the B&B lady comes to collect my plate, she looks offended: 'Nothing wrong with them, I hope?' Widening her eyes, she tells me to dip them into the fried egg.

I leave the dining room as soon as her back is turned, feeling I have escaped some deadly infection. But later that day, wandering through the town, I remember the invitation in her eyes and can't help wondering what she has done with the untouched breakfast.

Labour
For Justyna

Some old men were digging in the sun by a lane just outside town. Whenever a smiling couple strolled by, the old men stopped for a moment, rested on their spades, and nodded hello. As I approached, I thought I could see tears in their eyes and I tried to look the other way. But they called out and offered me a spade. And having nowhere to go, I took it, and was no longer young.

Division

They were going to cut the huge park in Rome in half. They would push the southern part out to sea to cut if off from the richer north. I found myself in the park as it was happening. Luckily I was just in the right half, but a friend I was meeting up with for the first time in ages had his feet on the other side. All I had wanted was to explore the eternal city, or at least its shadows on the hills.

Rome

Early each morning in the eternal city, I carried a knotted handkerchief full of sand so that I could feel its weight in my palm. In this way, I wouldn't forget where I'd come from. But then I'd pour the sand onto the pavement to remind myself I was free each morning to choose my life anew.

With my empty handkerchief back in my pocket, I would go to the café on the corner for a black coffee. There was never anyone in there at that time, apart from the owner and his wife, neither of whom seemed in a hurry to serve me.

Find

Seeing that I was lost, the travellers invited me to come and live with them. But would they understand my need to be alone? As if to tempt me further and at the same time confirm my fears, they pushed a small, dark-eyed woman towards me. She buried her face in my chest as if she were a bird trying to hide.

Provincial

It was a bright spring day. Turin's Via Roma was packed with shoppers. Strange, I thought, how in a few hours it would be dark and deserted. A part of me was hoping I would bump into my ex-wife, however unlikely that was. At the same time, I dreaded the prospect – she would see I was on my own and pity me.

I went into a bar. It was cool and quiet. The youth who handed me my beer spoke in English, telling me he had worked in New York the year before.

'At least there the streets are full of people at night as well during the day,' I said although I'd never been there.

The youth said nothing. Perhaps he did not wish to shame me by bringing my ignorance to light.

Last Trip

My mother had a metal brace attached to one leg. She tried, but couldn't get up the steps of the seaside train with the open roof, and I had to lift her. She was so light it was as if she were already spirit.

Cottage

I turn around to see my mother on the roof, clinging to a chimney. How did she get there? She's shouting down instructions: which apples to pick from the orchard behind me. And then, as if waking from a dream, she looks around in disbelief. *Catch me*, she cries, losing her grip. Now my father appears in the doorway, mouth wide open, hands stretched out. How can he be here? I thought he was dead. He's blushing with shame. We're both too late to rescue my mother.

Youth

Our true happiness only comes when the party is over, when we're free to wander dark deserted streets, with nothing to stop us dissolving into the night.

Morning After

I wake to find the house has fallen apart. I'm lying in bed exposed to the street. 'What happened?' I shout to my wife. She is sitting on the toilet, in the fresh air, laughing.

Opening

Fiddling in my old jacket, I accidentally found another pocket in the lining, one I never knew was there, just when I thought I'd already turned everything inside-out.

Corridor

This door opens into a room containing a replica of life exactly as it is. Except here everything has a limit to make us feel safe. Yet there are countless other doors opening into rooms we will never see. In the distance, the corridor grows smaller and smaller until it must come to an end – or open into that which we have no name for.

Care (1)

The woman in the wheelchair demanded I wheel her around the neat gardens of the posh hotel. Under her orders, I went faster and faster until I made myself so dizzy I collapsed, pulling the wheelchair down with me, so that she tumbled into my arms, the warmth and softness of her against me as we lay on the wet grass, with the world spinning.

Old Town

Through the window of the haberdashery, I saw two old friends of mine, Barbara and Janine. I hadn't seen them for a long time, and went inside to say hello, but they were busy talking to the salesman, both at the same time. They weren't quite sure of the type of button they wanted to buy for a particular coat, which they couldn't remember the name of. The young, lanky salesman was flirtatious and condescending with them at the same time. Eventually, in a bit of a huff, they left without buying anything or even noticing me.

I caught up with them in the piazza. They seemed unsure of who I was. Maybe a drink would jog their memories, I suggested. They told me they were busy, maybe another time.

Perhaps they were going to the fair up on the hill later on? We could ride the waltzers together just as we did in the old days.

They looked at each other, linked arms, and walked away, soon to be lost in the crowd.

To get to the fair, I had to climb a steep path. The town looked further and further away down below. It was a beautiful sunny day. I should be feeling much better about life, I told myself.

Lesson

Up in the mountains, seeking the truth about some incident that had taken place there many years before, I found myself wrestling with a fifteen-year-old shepherd. He was getting the better of me.

'Just think,' I cried, 'a fifteen-year old boy wrestling with a fifty-year old man!' At that he relented, not having realised how old I was.

It was then that I saw his mother. We hadn't made love in ages. We would have to get to know each other all over again.

I was prepared to take the initiative, but now the boy's father was approaching – perhaps to tell me, I thought, that I was going about the whole thing in the wrong way.

View

I had forgotten how difficult it was to get to the entrance of my old house in Naples. A sloping alleyway eventually turned into a tunnel hewn into the rocks many centuries before. The tunnel grew lower and narrower until I was forced to wriggle along like a worm. When I eventually arrived at the centuries-old door, I had to reach up with one hand through a narrow gap in the rock and with a huge rusty key feel my way to the lock, and then crawl in.

Inside, the ancient, dusty furniture was as I'd left it, but at the back was an orchard full of newly-fallen pink blossom lying in waves on the ground. It was a kind of foretaste of the sea.

As I was wondering whether this made the rest of my life worthwhile, a breeze sprang up and there was a fresh shower of blossom. I took a dozen snapshots of it on my iPhone to send back to my family in England, but the results were blurry and looked more like a painting than the kind of photo they were used to seeing.

Loss

One day on the crowded street, I came across a woman who'd been my lover years before. She wanted me to tell her all about my life since we'd parted. That same day, I chanced upon another woman, a stranger who said we should get to know one another. I told each of them I had a wife, although it didn't seem very real when I said it. They both expressed a desire to meet her, but that would mean letting them into my life, and I had no idea what that was anymore.

That Morning

I had no coins to give the homeless woman who held out her palm for money, so I invited her to the office where I worked. Since it was almost Christmas, I was sure my colleagues would be happy to chip in with some small change. That was my first mistake.

The second was when I realised she was someone who had once been at school with me. Wouldn't she tell us the story of her life, I asked her, and how she had ended up like this after her dreams of becoming somebody famous?

The third was when I burst into tears at the thought that after all these years I myself had no idea what I was doing in this office.

As my colleagues stared, the woman came over to me and pushed my chair on its wheels gently back and forth, singing the softest of lullabies as if she were soothing her own small child.

Family Affair

When I returned home after a year away, my mother and stepfather had moved house.

'What are all those flies doing here?' I asked, pointing to a corner of the kitchen ceiling. My mother and stepfather stared in the direction of my finger.

I took a fat Russian novel from the front pocket of my rucksack and began batting the flies, but they simply flew off and settled in another place. There seemed to be more and more of them. My stepfather looked at me as if I had brought the flies from abroad.

After a small search, I found an anti-insect spray and went outside to see how the flies were getting in. There was a hole just below the guttering, hidden behind a gas pipe.

If you buy a house, I thought, you really should check the outside as well as the inside. I squirted the little black bodies piling into the hole, and a giant flame shot up.

'What on earth is in that spray?' shouted my stepfather. 'Now we'll have to call the fire brigade.'

He stared at me and waited for my mother to dial 999.

Fields

We went to visit my brother who still lived in the tiny village where I grew up. To get to the nearest pub you had to drive down a lane for two miles or you could walk across the fields. My wife went with my brother in his beaten up old jalopy. My young daughter said she would walk with me, and I could show her some of the places where I used to play.

On the way, we came across some children throwing a stick for a dog. I remembered that once when walking alone here as a boy I was chased by another boy with a stick. I felt scared that these children would attack me and my daughter, though I knew my fear was ridiculous because I was a fully-grown man.

But now one of the boys was walking towards us with a stick and waving it. Though small and weedy, he had a vicious look.

My daughter started to cry. 'Stop that,' I said.

Then she began to really sob, tears streaming down her face. I grabbed her hand, and we ran away across the fields until we reached a farmyard. The farmer's wife came out of the house and wanted to know what was going on.

Country Holiday

On the first morning, I woke up too early. My wife and children were fast asleep, so I went for a walk on my own. Wandering through the fields and woods, I soon realised I didn't know my way back. It was so lovely, I didn't mind, but I hadn't had breakfast, and my wife might worry. I stopped off at a small farm to ask for directions. The farmer said there would be a bus along the lane in just a few minutes. He even gave me a few coins for the bus fare since I had left my wallet in the B&B.

On the backseat of the bus, there were two girls. One of them looked as if she must be the farmer's daughter, for she had the same ruddy cheeks and bright blue eyes. I sat a couple of rows down from them and heard the other girl saying how she had lost her boyfriend. When she started to cry, the farmer's daughter told her that I might be able to offer some consolation since I knew how it felt to be lost.

Pattern

The woman in the tourist office showed me a series of lit-up lines on an electronic map display. These represented interconnected shortcuts through the town. But I got lost and ended up on a path going through a field. Some white horses were grazing in a corner. I could feel a wind on my face and soon dark clouds began to appear. There was a clap of thunder not far away. The horses grew restless and ran towards me, so I climbed over a fence into a copse for safety. Then I heard a shout and turned to see a farmer approaching. I thought he was going to tell me off for being on his property, but he only wanted to warn me of the danger of being near trees when lightning struck, although their branches made a beautiful pattern against the sky, especially when there was a storm.

Visitor

I didn't expect the climb to be so difficult. The old woman in the village had told me it was part of any decent visitor's itinerary. Yet the hill got so steep towards the top that I had to cling onto tufts of grass and press my body hard against the surface to stop myself sliding down. Eventually I reached the summit, though I had to sit with my arms around a rock because of the wind sweeping over me in waves. The promised panoramic view was of nothing more than other hills similar to the one I was sitting on, where I was happy to be alone, though I had no idea how I'd get back down to the village.

Patronage

I took my seat on a bale in the barn where all the presentations were going on. In my trouser pocket I had some coins ready to donate to the speakers at the end. But the coins kept rolling out through a hole onto the concrete floor, making a terrible clatter. The man from India next to me, who had been so kind and deferential when I sat down, now regarded me with irritation and disdain.

    I noticed he had a gammy leg, and to make up to him, I offered to give him a lift to the poetry reading in the church later. Otherwise, I told him, he would have to negotiate a difficult path along the top of a steep slope, although there were trees to grab onto in case he slipped.

Tunnel

I was impressed by the man that I met on the train: his knowledge, his culture, his air of authority. But then he interrupted himself mid-sentence, got down on his knees by the train window and looked out, even though we were going through a tunnel. He asked me to kneel with him. He did not want me to pray, he said – he was not as unenlightened as that – but simply to be illuminated by the infinity of the moment. If I knelt down beside him, I would feel the light stream onto my face when the train emerged from the darkness. I did what he wanted, but all the time I couldn't shake off the feeling that he was more interested in converting me to his way of thinking than in liberating me.

Being Free

I entered the tunnel in search of the treasure hidden in a deep cave. The tunnel grew smaller and smaller until I was wriggling along on my front. Then my headlamp stopped working. The treasure could not be too far away, but I panicked at the thought of being lost or trapped. In the darkness I reversed until I was able to turn and flee back out into the sunlight. Here I wept with the joy of being free, but also with grief over what I had left undiscovered.

Lines

On my way to give a reading, I had to change trains at a small station by the sea. Here I was met by the poet P. He wanted to make sure I was qualified and that I really was on my way since I'd proved unreliable in the past. Yet he trusted me enough to hand over some passports of other poets he had invited, too. He asked if I would be so kind as to take them to Administration for photocopying when I arrived. New regulations, he explained. Once on the train, I flicked absentmindedly through the passports. I realised that they all belonged to friends of mine who lived in other countries, some of whom I hadn't seen for decades. What kind of a test was this?

My mobile rang. It was my mother. She was crying because she was worried I would forget my lines. With her dementia, she knew what that was like.

'It's a reading, not a play,' I said, looking out of the window at the crashing waves just a few yards from the railway track. But that only made her cry harder because she realised she didn't understand what was going on anymore.

Interruption

It took me ages to find the information desk in the crowded station concourse. Here, in bright red uniform, was my old girlfriend Jane, whom I hadn't seen for years. But she was chatting on the phone and paid me no attention. Did she even know who I was? It was only when I coughed that she looked over the counter in my direction. 'Ah, it's you…' she said, and would have gone straight back to her phone conversation if I hadn't insisted on her doing her job and finding out what had happened to my train.

Company (1)

In the south of France, a bar owner is helping me with corrections to my translation of Max Jacob's *Le Cornet à dés*. I am half-drunk on his red wine most of the time, and sometimes mix English, French and Italian in a single sentence. The locals indulge me because of my black-and-white cat, who smuggled herself into the boot of my car when I left England. They feed her all kinds of exotic dishes I don't think she would ever eat at home.

Worth

Over an aperitif with a French friend, I was talking about translating Max Jacob's *The Dice Cup* into English. If only someone were happy to pay me, I told him, I would do it. Otherwise, this was not an enterprise I wished to undertake. Yet the book deserved to be translated in its entirety, for not enough people knew of Jacob's prose poems.

Then the poet P. walked in with *his* French friend. He lifted his chin in the air when he saw me and frowned. *His* companion was the real French friend, his look implied, not mine.

'You've had a haircut,' he sneered, but did he despise the cheapness of it, or the fact that I had waited so long to have one?

Taint

In the French restaurant, there was a sophisticated array of dishes to choose from, but I didn't know what most of them were. I chose *soupe à l'oignon* as a first course, unsure whether to pronounce the 's' as more of a 'z'. The French restaurateur looked at me with disdain – the typical lazy choice of an Englishman. So for my main course I pointed at a fish dish I'd never heard of. The restaurateur made a smacking sound with his lips. A perfect choice, he said: the fish came from an area where a volcano gave it a unique flavour. When the fish was brought to me, all I could taste was ash. It lingered in my mouth for days.

Picnic

My German students asked about the ring my mother had given me before she died. Where had it gone, they wanted to know. I couldn't remember how I'd lost it. They looked astonished at such carelessness, but changed the subject, and opened the picnic hamper. It was packed full with bottles of white wine, bread rolls and an assortment of cold meats. It was lovely but overwhelmingly formal. Every now and again they would say something in German and laugh. Then they would apologise for speaking in German, but never explain what the joke was.

Verboten

In the German cinema, a man stood up and lit a cigarette, seemingly oblivious of the rules and regulations, and of the rest of the audience, none of whom dared reproach him. Then, from the darkness, a fire hose emerged, though one couldn't see the hand behind it, and fired a stream of water into the man's chest. He looked as if he might fall, but after a few moments he recovered and cursed the fire hose, officialdom and the cowardice of the people. Defiantly, he lit another cigarette, but it only took a couple of puffs for the invisible hand to push the fire hose forward once more and shoot out a terrifyingly powerful stream. This time the man writhed with the shock of it, yet still he was able to stop himself from falling. He shook his fist at the withdrawing hose and once again took out his packet of cigarettes. But now it was soaked through, so he hurled it into the darkness where the fire hose was hidden. Still no one said a word.

Reception

When I was invited to a big wedding in Italy, I didn't know if they had booked me into the Albergo Falcone, which I remembered from a previous visit was not very clean, or the Hotel Milano, which was more corporate, but had a reputation for ripping people off.

I asked the thin, elegant man at the Hotel Milano reception if there was a reservation for me and what the price was. He eyed me up and down. My being fussy with money was a clear sign that I didn't have much of it, and even worse did not have the good manners to conceal the fact. Or perhaps his look was simply a way to put pressure on me to pay more in order to prove him wrong.

At that moment, a party of guests arrived. The man turned to them, as if I didn't exist. I should have walked out and gone across the road to the Albergo Falcone, but what if they didn't have any rooms? I would have the embarrassment of returning here, and the man at reception, seeing my desperation, would hike the price up still further.

Abuse

In the Turin bank, I noticed an English woman – pretty in a thin and pale way – having trouble at the counter. I offered to translate for her. We got into conversation and it turned out that she, like me, was from Lancaster and knew Father K., whom I had once worked for as a volunteer in a centre for the homeless.

'Is he still alive?' I asked, knowing he would not be. 'No,' she said. 'He was very ill, you know.'

I remembered him having to have both legs removed at the knee because of diabetes. 'A good and brave man,' she said.

I said nothing. What came to mind was Father K.'s grim smile of satisfaction when he told me how as a headmaster he would cane boys until they begged for mercy. 'It's for their own good,' he used to say.

Taking me for a Catholic, she invited me to visit a nearby church with her. I went only because I fancied my chances, forgetting I would have to dip my fingers into the holy water and make the sign of the cross before I entered.

Translator

I couldn't stand my job at Olivetti anymore. I typed up my notice and handed it in. An HR committee summoned me to a posh meeting room to ask why I was leaving. It was obvious from their weary voices and mechanical gestures that they were just going through the motions. After all, I had resigned once before and returned after only a few months. There would be no coming back this time, they warned me.

That same evening, I regretted my decision. I was now settled in Italy and would be uprooted all over again if I couldn't find another job here. I called up an old supervisor, someone who had always looked out for me. I asked him if he thought it was not too late to change my mind. He said he would find out through the grapevine. A couple of hours later, he rang back and told me the committee would be happy, as he put it, to press the reset button. It would make life easier for them too. However, for the sake of protocol, I would have to write a letter in Italian formally withdrawing my resignation.

Just the thought of sitting once again at my computer to type another letter made me feel exhausted. Better to close my eyes and let things happen as they would, though I was sure to wake with a jolt.

Job

I was sent to Moscow, but had no idea where I was going to stay. My Russian colleague took me through the streets at night. We bumped into a drunk, who challenged me to a fight to see who was more 'manly'. It ended up like a game of tag because he was too far gone to land a punch.

When we'd got rid of him, I asked my colleague where I would stay. He told me not to worry. We're were going to have a good time.

We ended up walking through the rubble of torn down blocks of flats. I wondered whether it was worth carrying a gun, but my colleague told me to think about the consequences of doing so. Soon everyone would be carrying one.

He took me to a packed cocktail bar. A woman in a red dress asked if I would buy her a drink. She pressed her hip against mine and smiled, though her eyes looked dead. I could see my colleague, as if from a distance, disappearing into the crowd.

Bad Breath

After the accident, I was wheeled around by a nurse. Just the sight of her full lips gave me an erection, which I tried in vain to hide under my blanket.

One day a rough-looking man and a little boy with a tiny lame dog overtook us on a country lane. The boy eyed me contemptuously. I thought he was even going to hit me with his stick (twice the size he was), but the lame dog took a shine to me and rubbed itself against the side of my shin. So the boy decided to walk close by me, too. The man turned and looked back at us with impatience, but I could see from his half-smile that he was glad the boy had finally found another friend besides the dog.

The nurse was so pleased she bent over to give me a first kiss, though she wrinkled her nose with disgust when her lips met mine.

Inheritance

A professional woman lived in the flat above mine. I was on my own, out of work, and often behind with the rent. She kept her distance. A small plant someone had given me for Christmas kept me company.

One day I came into some money and was able to buy the flat. Meanwhile, the small plant had grown into a tree whose branches were pushing against the ceiling, threatening to break through into the flat of the woman, who still kept her distance.

Precious

Behind the counter, in a glass-fronted bookcase, were some antique volumes of Shelley and Byron. The Romantic poets had been as popular as rock stars once; now so many of their works turned up in second-hand bookshops. The man at the till asked if I was interested in purchasing one of them. I assumed they were too expensive, so I settled for browsing through paperbacks instead, though there was nothing of interest.

A woman in a torn coat came in. She was trying to sell some copies of an autobiography she had in a filthy plastic bag, but the man told her to go away. I must have looked sympathetic, for she took me by the arm and told me she had written the book when she learnt that she was going to die from a congenital disease. There were only a few remaining copies and she wanted to sell them all in the little time she had left. She led me out into the rain and we hurried through the streets together in search of another second-hand bookshop.

Need

My wife was flipping through a magazine when I got into bed. Under the sheets, I felt something warm and furry between us. At first I thought it was our cat, but as I explored with my fingertips, it gave me a sharp nip. I pulled back the duvet. A tiny puppy.

How did that get here? I asked.

My wife shrugged and went back to her reading.

Then I heard a soft whining from under the bed. A dog's head emerged. Its long ears looked as if they'd recently been chewed. By what? I wondered.

Then I felt something large pushing up against me from below. I jumped out of bed and peered underneath. A middle-aged woman in a torn coat was lying there. She had tears on her cheeks. I wanted to know what had happened, but instead of asking her, I told her to leave or I'd call the police.

My wife turned over another page of her magazine, with only the briefest of glances in my direction.

Care (2)

When I came back from holiday, the door to my flat was broken open and there was a small boy on the sofa in my front room watching television. He told me he was an orphan and meant no harm. His eyes looked pitiful, but a small smile played around his lips. I wondered how I could look after him when I had my own life to get on with. However, it was starting to rain and I couldn't throw him out now. Besides, he looked hungry. I remembered I had a sandwich left over in my rucksack, but before I could give it to him, he snatched it out of my hand.

Investment

The taxi driver with a strange accent wouldn't leave me alone. When he took me somewhere, he didn't just drop me off, but waited, hours if needs be, to bring me back home. He only wanted to be my friend, he said.

At that time, I had a small puppy. Once when I was taking it for a walk and throwing twigs for it to fetch, the taxi driver drew up beside me. He rolled down his window and told me I was wasting my time. I could be doing something useful, he said. Chatting to him would be better than throwing a twig for a puppy. One day, he told me, his friendship would no longer be available, for he planned to return to his own country as soon as he had made enough money to build a house there.

I didn't see how he would ever make enough money if he spent all his time hanging around me.

The Unseen Everyday

For the first time, I was going to be late at the school in Turin where I taught English as a foreign language. The city looked different this morning. The streets and squares were bathed in a beautiful, yet somehow ominous golden glow, which had so distracted me that I was now lost. I was standing in front of a huge bookshop I had never seen before. There were books of philosophy with ancient lettering in the window. A hunched old man with rimless spectacles was just unlocking the door, and even though by now I should have already been with my pupils, I couldn't resist his invitation to step inside. Books in different languages lay on shelves that seemed to stretch into the distance. I wandered along them until I found myself alone in semi-darkness, where a chance reach brought me a book entitled *The Unseen Everyday*. Even before opening its heavy covers, I sensed that here was a text which would finally illuminate my understanding of the life beyond life and yet within the life itself that I led, although it would never enable me to find my way around the city or arrive on time.

Business

I was sent to a city on the southern edge of Morocco. After a while, my wife came out to join me. As soon as I could, I took her through hot deserted streets to show her the city's ancient beauty. Near the top of a steep alleyway, she was desperate for a pee. Not here, I begged her. Do you want me to pee in my knickers? she said. A Moroccan youth at the bottom of the alley spotted us. Quick, get up, I said. I can't, she said, I have to finish. Some men joined the youth. They pointed up at us and laughed, but the laughter had anger in it. I led my wife by another alleyway back to the hotel. I hoped they would not follow us, but a large crowd soon gathered outside and began to shout and shake their fists. It was no use trying to hide – that would only make them worse. In spite of my wife's protests, I went outside to try and explain that in our culture it was not such a terrible mark of disrespect to pee in the street if you had to and if no one else was around. In response, the youth challenged me to a wrestling match. I was taller than him, but he was stockier and much fitter. Yet in our struggle, I was surprised at how strong I became through sheer necessity. I found joy in this discovery and soon my fear had gone. When some soldiers arrived to break us up and disperse the crowd, I was disappointed as well as relieved.

Distances

Each time I meet my father it is in a different city, but we always stumble across a second-hand bookshop and go inside. He likes it when I ask the bookshop owner where the poetry section is. 'Still reading poetry, then?' he says with a smile. In truth, I am only interested in seeing if they have something by the Scottish poet Alan Jackson. My father once gave me a battered, stained copy of Jackson's first pamphlet *Underwater Wedding*. It was when I went to see him after his separation from my mother. I was still a teenager, but the pamphlet kept me company for years on my travels until I lost it on a train somewhere between Paris and Turin. I have never found another copy, none of the bookshop owners has heard of *Underwater Wedding*, and my father says he has no recollection of such a title.

Survival

I wasn't sure I'd remember the path. I was walking with my daughter through a forest in search of the ruins of a cottage where I used to hide when I ran away from home. If only I'd known on those cold nights that years later I'd return with my own flesh and blood to discover that the old blanket I slept in was still there.

Together

There were two of our daughter, and my husband wanted to kill both of them to make her come back to life as one. While I held each of my daughter down, my husband wielded the knife, blood on both our faces. Our daughter returned whole but still my husband wasn't happy. He wanted to kill her again and bring her back as someone else, yet recognisable as ours. Once more I went to hold her down, but this time she fled because a part of her remembered what we'd done before.

Mauvaise Foi

They instruct me to walk from the skyline to the centre of the city, just as I did years ago. The film they made of me then has faded to the point where it can no longer be restored. The challenge with this new film, they say, is not to look disheartened as I did as a youth, when to be gloomy was a sign of existentialist faith, but to wear a corporate smile, and to make it seem authentic.

Company (2)

Walking around the town with my colleagues after a dinner with wine, I find I'm enjoying it more than I thought I would. The anxiety which has plagued me for years has gone; my confidence is back. Perhaps that's because our new boss is cracking jokes in his loud American voice. Then, as we turn a corner into the packed main street, I am overwhelmed by a sense of time slipping by, of having missed something vital. I want to sneak away without a word and make my way alone until I can hear my own thoughts, perhaps step into the second-hand bookshop we passed without a glance a few minutes ago. But I keep pace with my colleagues, keep laughing at the boss's jokes.

Company (3)

I only called on her because I happened to pass that way. All was fine as we sat on cushions on the floor, hippy-style, though we both worked in an office. Over a bottle of wine, we talked about art, poetry and music, as well as exchanging bits of office gossip. It started to go wrong when I said, '1956 was the most important year.' She looked at me, waiting for me to go on.

'It was the year of the Suez crisis, and it was the year Elvis made his entrance onto the world stage.'

She frowned when I said this.

'Of course, he'd been in music for a couple of years already, but 1956 was the year in which he became truly famous. Besides,' I went on, 'it was the year I was born.' I raised a toast, which she did not return.

So I said goodbye and started to make my way across town. Coming around a corner into a street which was usually lined with hookers but was now deserted, I saw a light brown hamster sniffing from left to right. It didn't seem at all startled by me and even let me pick it up. I wondered if it belonged to someone nearby or if I could take it home with me. Better, I thought, to leave it where it was, although I would only regret doing so when I got back to my empty room.

Historical Movie

I had been flirting with the leading lady for some time. When she put on the Anglo-Saxon tunic, I went one step further. I took her in my arms, kissed her, then slid my hands down over the coarse material to her bottom.

'Mmm, I bet it's much softer underneath,' I said, squeezing.

This was not in the script, but she returned my kiss as if still playing her part, while the camera crew filmed on with sly approval.

Earlier that day I had travelled with the poet P. by train. Across the aisle was a man who looked like Yeats, and who was reading a biography of Yeats with a picture of Yeats on the cover.

'He must be Yeats's great niece,' I whispered to the poet P.

I had meant to say 'nephew'. P. looked at me as if I were an idiot. Too late now to impress him with the sheaf of poems I had brought with me.

But here he was arriving on the film set, staring at my hands, no doubt wondering where they were going next.

Want

She told me she hadn't really wanted to make love with me all those years ago. She'd just been too weary to say no. But didn't you like it when I kissed you on the throat? I asked, and bent down to kiss her there again. She didn't move away, nor did she respond, just like the first time, I now remembered.

Kiss

I was on my hotel room balcony watching the holiday makers by the swimming pool, in particular a woman with whom I'd exchanged smiles the evening before. She was playing in the water with her child, who was shrieking with delight. I was about to go back to my book when she shielded her eyes from the sun and waved up to me. I waved back. A little later there was a knock at the door. When she kissed me in the open doorway, I was so surprised I stepped back. 'What's the matter? Don't you like me?' she wanted to know. 'It's not that. In fact, you're perfect,' I said, wondering what she'd done with the child.

Arrival

It was late. The hotels were all full. The only place I could stay the night was a hostel for migrants – a one-roomed flat in a tall, crumbling block. I was scared I'd be robbed, but the migrants only looked at me with a kind of childlike curiosity, even sympathy.

The next day I found a hotel, but felt compelled to return to where I'd spent the night to see if I could help in any way. I remembered that the flat was on the thirty-fourth floor, but now I could only find the thirty-third and thirty-fifth floor. There was no floor in between. I went up and down the block, feeling more and more panicky, the residents opening their doors with angry faces because of the disturbance I was causing.

The Order of Things

Now that he had arrived in Paris, the refugee wanted to make a call back to his home country. I took him along to the telephone exchange. A tall, thin clerk told me that the man still owed a seven-euro supplementary charge from his last call. While I was querying this, the refugee pushed open a fire-door, and set off the alarm. We both ran out after him, but he was already sprinting down the street at a pace we could never hope to match. I was afraid the clerk would bring the force of his bureaucratic anger to bear on me, but I was prepared to stand my ground. Instead, the clerk ridiculed the fleeing refugee by starting to run on the spot, knees high, arms pumping the air like a puppet's, pretending to be out of breath, a supercilious smile on his bony face.

Spring Morning

The youth on the early morning bus down from the hills was very chatty. He spoke to me with the trace of an eastern European accent, and was charming, almost flirtatious with it.

There were only two other passengers.

A plump, middle-aged man in a suit which was too small for him said he worked for a department store, and that he could get the youth a job there.

'Will he be given a uniform?' I asked.

'No, he'll have to buy that himself,' the man said.

'Oh, I think he should be given one,' I said.

'But if he is prepared to buy his own uniform, then that will be a sign of proper commitment,' the man said.

The other passenger, who looked like a farmer's wife, nodded in agreement.

'Where are you from?' I asked the boy, 'and how long have you been in this country?'

'You shouldn't ask him that,' said the woman, 'it's racist.'

'I'm not racist,' I said, 'I lived in France for a year, in Italy for two years, and in Poland for three. People were always asking me where I was from.'

'I still think it's racist,' the woman said.

The man was frowning for he had still not acquired a commitment from the boy, and our argument was not helping matters.

Dialogue

I told her that if she didn't speak to me in Italian, my Italian would grow so rusty I might forget how to speak it altogether.

Then I told her that if she didn't kiss me, I might forget how to kiss.

So, a little reluctantly at first, she spoke to me in Italian, kissed me and then kissed me some more.

I discovered that she had once been a student at the language school where I used to teach. Did she know Dave? I asked her. Dave who? she said.

I can't remember, I said, but he had a brother called John.

Romance

I walked with my Italian friend to the beginning of the path which led from the river up a steep hill covered in pine trees to the border of Switzerland. It was time for us to say goodbye. At the other end, a Swiss boy she had met earlier in the summer would be waiting for her. My friend was wondering if she had enough clothes in her small rucksack. Perhaps she should have taken her elegant cardigan. But then she wondered if a Swiss boy would appreciate its delicate blue. Perhaps he wouldn't even be waiting for her anyway. They'd only had the briefest of romances on the Italian Riviera. 'You can come back if he's not there,' I said, 'back down the path between the trees. At least it will still be sunny here.' But she was worried what the people in our village would think of her if she returned so soon. 'You could come and live with me,' I said, although I knew that wasn't true.

Light

One spring dawn, I heard someone outside singing the most beautiful song I had ever heard in a language which sounded as if it came from another time. I got up and pulled back the curtains. Through the window, I could see a youth walking across the dewy field at the back of our house. Although I was afraid, I couldn't resist waving. With a gesture he invited me to come out and join him, and I knew he would not mock me if I sang along with him, although I had no idea what it was I was meant to sing.

Hike

When my father and I stopped our hike for a break, I couldn't resist opening my rucksack and taking out the first few pages of a long poem in progress. But as soon as I started reading it to him, his perpetual frown grew deeper, and I realised I'd made a mistake. It was like someone exposing a film too soon to the light. We were sitting on the side of a mountain. The sun would go down before we knew it. There was still a long way to go.

Daybreak

The man emerges from the forest into a dewy field. He's dressed in a coat which has long since lost its colour. The sky is for the moment clear, on its way to becoming bright. After a walk across fields, he comes to a cottage. The man's hungry, cold, but afraid to knock. What kind of greeting, if any, will he receive? Perhaps further along there will be other houses, and he will be less afraid. So he walks down a steep lane, at the end of which is a cluster of houses.

He decides not to beg for something to eat and drink, but instead pretend he only wants to ask the way to the nearest town. Then someone might understand and invite him into the warmth of their home.

Oh, but then he will have to talk and explain who he is, but this he has forgotten, and is afraid to discover.

He comes to a bus-stop and feels in his pockets. A few coins. Perhaps enough for a bus to somewhere bigger, even a city. But there will be so many like him in a city.

Now the bus is here, its doors are opening. The driver is asking him where he wants to go.

The answer will come to him, it will come to him.

Incomplete

It was an event to celebrate something, but I could no longer remember what. 'What's going on?' I asked a colleague.

He looked at me. 'What do you mean, what's going on?'

'I'm sorry, I'm really not myself today,' I said.

'Why don't you go into the refreshment room?' he suggested, pointing to a door.

The only person in there – it was really just a dilapidated storeroom – was the woman from IT, famous for her stammer. She was standing by a small window, gazing out.

I went over to join her, wondering what there was to look at. Not much, as it turned out. Just a backyard with a couple of overflowing bins.

'Oh, it's y-you,' she said, not looking at me, but putting her head on my shoulder as if she'd done so a thousand times before.

The event, whatever it was, was sure to be a waste of time, but at least now there was the possibility of romance.

Poem

For years, I worked as a technical translator from Norwegian into English. One day my employer gave me a poem to translate. It was written in tercets. A welcome change, I thought, and got up to go to the coffee machine to celebrate. 'This is only the first page,' he said, bringing out a fat sheaf of papers from his briefcase, 'of an epic poem written by Knut Hamsun, Norway's answer to Dante.'

That evening I went to an authors' party. They were discussing whether or not it was possible to still make a living from writing. Not if you write the kind of poetry I was translating, I thought.

Returning home down an alleyway, I saw a man coming towards me. He seemed somehow familiar and when he passed me, I recognised him as a former colleague. He was wearing a cheap, crumpled suit, and stank of whiskey. I was going to say hello, but he was staring at the ground, and I didn't wish to startle him.

When I told my wife about my day, she grew impatient. 'That's hardly a story worth the telling,' she said.

Destination

It was hot and dusty. I'd fallen asleep on the train and only woken up just in time to get off at the small country station where I had to change trains. My shoelaces were untied, my belt undone, and my overstuffed suitcase had sprung open so that I had to carry it flat in my hands. My train to the sea and a new life was just a little further up the empty platform. But there was no one else on the train, not even the driver.

Separation

Free now, I wondered where I could live without being thought of as useless and strange. Perhaps in Rome I would find work explaining to foreigners the meaning of pictures for sale along the river embankment, some of which had been painted by an Italian friend before we lost touch. To be sure, having cut all ties, I would be drifting for however long it took towards my death, no longer believing in the promise of the new life I used to dream of.

Invitation

My old school-friend found out where I was living abroad. He sent me a card inviting me, the next time I was in the country, to visit him at his farmhouse. It was starting to get dark when I arrived at the gate. I could see him through the kitchen window, setting the table where I used to sit and drink fresh milk from the farm with him. He still moved with a farm boy's agility, and had the same curls in his hair, though all its brown had gone. I so much wanted to hear the story of his life, and to tell him the story of mine. Yet I remained at the gate, afraid we would no longer be able to grasp what was true just by looking each other in the eye.

In the Empty House

We found what looked like a piece of light, unmoving, frozen in the shape of a human being. We were afraid to touch it – it looked cold enough to burn us. What would happen if we could unfreeze it? Would it melt and vanish, or would it keep its shape and come alive? Could we take it away with us? Would it make any difference to how we lived, or loved, one way or another?

Mud, Gold

A stranger told me there was another city on the other side of the one I knew, where there were giant statues of gold on the shoreline. But what route could I find to take me there? The stranger directed me to a bus-stop by a park where some youths were playing football. While I was waiting, one of them asked if I would play with them, just for a few minutes to make up a side until their mate got back. I didn't know how to say no, though I was afraid of missing the bus. Perhaps because of my age they seemed reluctant to tackle me the one time I had the ball, and I almost scored, but just as I was about to take a shot, I slipped and fell. When I got back to the stop, my backside covered in mud, a blind woman asked for my help in crossing the road. I couldn't say no. It was only afterwards as I was watching her walk away that I thought about inviting her to come and explore the city on the other side with me, even though the statues would be invisible to her.

Recognition

As we walked along the Seine, I was looking forward to showing the poet Jeremy Over around the Shakespeare bookshop. When we arrived, however, the tall thin man at the till apologised because all the shelves were covered in a yellowish plastic sheeting to protect the books from leaks in the roof. Nevertheless, he was kind enough to lead us to the 'New York' section, telling us that for just a few minutes we could lift up the sheeting. I whispered in Jeremy's ear that I believed the man was none other than the famous Ron Padgett, although he must have fallen on hard times to have to make his living in this way. Jeremy smiled. 'I know all about that,' he said. And then, in an almost apologetic tone: 'To be honest, he's invited me to do a reading here in a few days' time.' Yes, of course. Why did I imagine that Jeremy had never been here before? Indeed, now that I thought about it, I remembered he'd once told me that his own books were on sale in the shop, and that he'd already met Ron Padgett on several occasions. 'A few years ago, I did a reading here myself,' I told Jeremy, remembering as I spoke what a dismal affair it had been.

Vita Nova

Making a mental list of all the things I would do in my new life, I walked over the bridge to the Academy on the other side of the river. As I climbed the flight of steps to the entrance, from behind a narrow window a man with a face so white it looked as if it had never felt the sunlight watched me approach. How dared I imagine I was worthy of entering the Academy after all the upset I had caused over the years? I would have to explain that my making fun of the authorities had not sprung from any malice, only from a youthful sense of irreverence, which unfortunately had lasted well into middle age. Now I was going to make amends. When I pushed open the ancient door, I was surprised that no one was there. Yet as I wandered dark, deserted corridors, I could still feel the weight of the man's eyes upon me.

Good Behaviour

In spite of his age, the old ex-con had a boyish enthusiasm about climbing trees. It had been like that all his life, he said. The worst thing about being in prison was the lack of trees. A small crowd gathered at the side of the street to watch him climb one now. He was only halfway up when a police officer arrived and told us to move on. When I hesitated, he shoved me so hard I fell and hit my elbow. With a grin, the ex-con kept climbing.

Voice

Back in Pigalle, some of the decrepit little streets have been knocked down to make way for an upmarket residential area. One ancient café remains in its midst, however, where a tiny woman sings her heart out in a reedy voice. Everyone is watching her, except for her son. He is drawing up her will on scraps of paper, which he intends to distribute once the show is over. His handwriting is difficult to read, but one can still make out the odd word or phrase, such as 'lyrics', 'dress' and 'purse – with or without money'.

Telangiectasia

At the packed trade fair, I bumped into my old boss. He suggested we swop business cards so that we could arrange to meet for dinner. In contrast to my plain white one, his was designed in elegant vintage style with gold lettering on a background of dark blue sea. However, I saw that his surname was missing some letters. 'Bob Brooker' had become 'Bob Brook'. I was wondering whether to say something about this when he told me that on my card I was now 'Ian See'. Why hadn't I spotted this before?

'Anyway, you look well,' I told him. And he did. Beneath his now bald cranium, his eyes had retained their boyish eagerness, and his tailor-made suit showed off his athletic frame.

'You too,' he said, with some hesitation, looking me up and down. 'That is,' he went on, 'apart from the broken veins on your nose.'

I had noticed these myself in the mirror only the other day. They were spreading out and downward in tiny intersecting streams. They seemed to have come from nowhere, and I had no idea what to do about them.

The Road to the City

The Italian author N was by now in her nineties. When she autographed her latest book for me at the book fair, I wanted to thank her, and impress her too, by listing the titles of her earlier books; I'd read every one of them. '*The Road to the City* was your second book,' I began. 'What was my first?' she asked, rolling her wheelchair back from me a couple of feet as if to get a better look at me. I couldn't remember. Instead, I began to list the titles of all her other books, while she regarded me with increasing suspicion. It was like talking to my Italian ex, like trying to prove to her that my love for her was real, even if it was only now that it was too late I'd come to realise that, just as I would only come to remember the title of N's first book when the fair was over.

Block

When the train arrived at Ivrea station, the train doors wouldn't open. The guard came hurrying through the carriage to tell us that because of a technical hitch we weren't allowed to alight; the train would have to go on to Aosta, the next station. Aosta was in fact the previous station, not the next one, but the guard had already passed through to another carriage before I could ask him what he meant. We waited for the train to start moving, but nothing happened. It was starting to grow dark and the lights in the train weren't working. My companion, the poet P., didn't seem to notice. He was telling me about a famous Italian author he'd had an affair with on his last trip here. 'She doesn't put on any airs and graces,' he said. 'What's more, she understands the value of silence.' I wished the same could be said of him. He hadn't stopped talking since that morning, when we'd climbed a hill together and he was too out-of-breath to speak.

Soap

Here are some clips of the poet P. from over the decades. In each one he is talking about the 'Dantean epic' he is 'scrambling together', but no-one is holding their breath anymore.

Differences

'The Italians…' I started to say to the young Italian woman before she burst into a fit of giggles. When she'd calmed down, she explained to me that it was the 's' at the end of the word 'Italian', instead of 'i', as in 'Italiani', which she found so funny. The 's' made a strange hissing sound to her ears, as if implying an innate British distrust of foreigners. But it was she who had asked me about the differences between Italy and England, and I'd only wanted to answer politely. Sitting opposite her in the old-style train carriage, it occurred to me how lovely she looked in her summer dress, and her light-green eyes were full of curiosity.

Carriage

A baby with a black cat's head suckles on the breast of its mother, who is a nun with glasses and a withered face, sitting opposite me in a Virgin train carriage.

Pet

Among other animals, she kept a tiny monkey, which made its home in the kitchen, often covering itself with a tea towel and making a game of peeking out. When it jumped onto my shoulder, I was afraid it would bite me, yet it only gave my ear an affectionate nibble. But when it jumped from my shoulder into the hot washing-up water in the sink and disappeared in the soap bubbles, I was afraid it would scald itself, and I was annoyed that the owner had so carelessly left the water unattended. I fished the monkey out. It had gone all limp and so I put it under the cold tap to see if that would revive it. But now I realised that the kitchen window was open out onto the busy street, and the monkey was about to escape.

Suits

I spent most of my working life in the men's suit section of a posh department store. Then sales began to fall. Management decided they needed someone younger and I was pushed into retirement.

A few days later I snuck back and watched surreptitiously to see how my replacement was faring. She must have been barely out of school. To be sure, she was smart and polite, but you could see from her eyes she was just going through the motions. I considered offering her some help, but what if she thought I was just an old man molesting her?

And so I kept watching, disappointed that none of my former customers ever asked her what had happened to me.

Lock Keeper

The retired professor, whose position I now occupied, told me of some ancient paintings locked away in a cave. He entrusted me with a huge key, saying he had some business to sort out at the university. Would I be so kind as to fetch one of the paintings for him?

When I unlocked the centuries-old door, it was obvious that the paintings were fake. As if drawn by a small child, they depicted stickmen in small canoes rowing through choppy waters. Looking more closely, I saw that in one or two places the paint was still wet.

Back at my office, I found the professor happily typing at my computer. He'd cleared away all my books and replaced them with his own. I was about to remind him that he no longer worked here when I realised I'd left his key behind.

As I approached the cave again, I saw waves crashing out with tiny flailing men in them. I turned and fled to the top of a small hill, where there was a pub called The Lock Keeper, which the landlord assured me was open for business as usual.

Cry

As soon as I came into the school, the receptionist told me there was someone on the phone for me. Yet when she gave me the receiver all I could hear was a distant babble. 'Who is it?' I shouted. Then I became aware that I was holding the earpiece to my mouth. When I turned the receiver round, the voice became louder, but still I couldn't catch the words. Then I just made out, 'It's Donatella, your old student', and in that moment I saw her a few yards away from me. She was looking in the other direction. I called out to her, but she began to walk away, and the voice on the phone grew fainter and fainter until I could no longer see or hear her.

Academic

The reason his slide presentation was not convincing was that it was obvious he had no personal experience of the traumatic consequences of not following the rules of the case he was presenting. I could have offered to step onto the stage in his place, but that would have meant revealing my own vulnerabilities. When he'd finished, my ex-wife got up to give her presentation. I could see how shaky she was, how unsure of herself. Not untypical of a woman of my generation, it occurred to me. I would have liked to reassure her, but it was too late now.

Reading

I was surprised by the reflection in the hand-mirror she gave me before I went on stage. My eyebrows looked as if they'd been plucked to death. There were only a few strands of hair on my skull. I was old, almost ready to die, yet still so vain.

Complicit

She showed me a satirical portrait she'd sketched of me, in which I looked like a denizen of a house of ill-repute. She challenged me to replicate the drawing, but to paint myself in a different light, and to include her in the picture. The problem was I was no good at drawing, and only likely to make a bad situation worse. Useless to tell her I hadn't done anything wrong apart from live my life a little too distractedly at a time when what I did would alter her life too.

Illuminated

The poet P., among others, set me an exam in which I had to write about a famous artist, whose works I'd said I admired. He gave me no time to prepare and I couldn't remember the years in which the artist was born and died. Yet just as I thought I'd have to get up and abandon the exam room – a large hall in which I sat alone with my examiners – all kinds of poetic sentences about the artist and his work began to flow from my pen, seemingly without any bidding on my part. Towards the end of the exam, reviewing what I'd done, I was amazed to find I'd also painted some pictures in black and blue ink, which, although technically flawed, conveyed a strange ethereal beauty. And yet I was someone who had never in his life been able to draw or paint.

Game

Taking a shortcut through the fields, I pass some boys playing football. One of them, apart from the rest, chucks a clump of mud at me. He knows I can't touch him. He's only a boy. But I pick up the mud, pack it close and throw it back at him. He pretends to cry, then yells to his mates, 'Hey, see what this man's started!' I begin to walk away, then sense he's behind me and break into a run. I see myself from outside – a tall man fleeing from a small boy, who chases him with a piece of mud in one raised hand.

New Friend

I decided to take her to the house where I'd been renting a room for ages, though I'd never actually stayed there. It was so long since I'd been back that I felt obliged to ring the doorbell instead of using my key. The landlady took her time coming to the door, and greeted me with a brittle smile. I found my room unlocked, but there was nothing to steal anyway, apart from an ancient TV coated in dust. I was surprised, however, to find that in the tiny en-suite, the shower curtain was wet and there were pubic hairs on the toilet. But I couldn't say anything, not with my new friend here. She was the kind of person who'd want to see the sort of life I led, and she had no idea I wasn't really living there at all.

In My Absence

The tree in the piazza has grown beyond belief, its thick branches spread down and across as well as up. Like fat snakes they've engulfed the square. Why has nobody cut them away? I'm tired and want to sit down, but I'm afraid I'll fall asleep, and wake entangled.

Work

When I awoke, I looked out of the window and saw vineyards and hills stretching into the distance. I was on the wrong train. It was moving at the pace of someone walking.

I went to find the train conductor. He was sitting on the floor, reading a book of poetry, his conductor's jacket unbuttoned at the front. Standing over him, I asked him how I could get to Turin. He replied in a local dialect I found hard to follow that people took this train to commute to their job picking grapes.

'But does the train go to Turin eventually?' I asked.

He closed his book and stood up, brushing down his jacket. For the first time, his dreamy eyes met mine, but instead of answering he launched into a history of trains in the region, of how, in contrast to countries like England, they had remained an integral part of the landscape as well as the lives of those who belonged here.

While I had some sympathy with his otherworldliness, the fact remained that I was going to be late to an important interview.

I turned to a peasant woman sitting nearby, and as I did so an old Italian song came onto the speaker. She got up on her seat and invited me to jump up and dance with her. How could I refuse?

Criteria

I was interviewed by an Englishman, but he spoke to me in Italian to see if I knew the language as well as I claimed. I didn't think his Italian was as good as mine, and the conversation felt so stilted I found it difficult to find the right words. It was only as we were leaving the building together that we spoke in English.

'How was it?' I asked him

'All right,' he said, looking at me as if wondering whether to go on. 'You did make a couple of mistakes. For example, you used "criteria" as a plural noun. In Italian the plural is "criteri".'

'You made some mistakes yourself,' I hit back, although I couldn't remember what they were.

'This is where we say goodbye,' he said, turning into a side street.

I realised I had no idea where I was or how to get to the cheap hotel where I was staying near the station. What on earth had brought me back to this city after so many years?

A youth on a scooter stopped and asked if I was lost. He told me he would take me where I wanted to go. As we wove in and out of the traffic, I held fast to him, the warmth of his suede leather jacket against my cheek.

www.ingramcontent.com/pod-product-compliance
Lightning Source LLC
Chambersburg PA
CBHW031158160426
43193CB00008B/426